Your Complete Forecast 2018 Horoscope

VIRGO

Your Complete Forecast 2018 Horoscope

VIRGO

BEJAN DARUWALLA
With
NASTUR DARUWALLA

Ranvir Books
HARPER element

First published in India in 2017 by Harper Element
An imprint of HarperCollins *Publishers*

P-ISBN: 978-93-5277-340-4
E-ISBN: 978-93-5277-341-1

2 4 6 8 10 9 7 5 3 1

HarperCollins *Publishers*
A-75, Sector 57, Noida, Uttar Pradesh 201301, India
1 London Bridge Street, London, SE1 9GF, United Kingdom
2 Bloor Street East, Toronto, Ontario M4W 1A8, Canada
Lvl 13, 201 Elizabeth Street (PO Box A565, NSW, 1235), Sydney
NSW 2000, Australia
195 Broadway, New York, NY 10007, USA

Typeset in 11.5/15 Sabon
By Saanvi Graphics, Noida

Printed and bound at
MicroPrints (India), New Delhi

Contents

VIRGO

23 August–22 September

Virgo is reserved, modest, practical, discriminating and industrious, analytical and painstaking, seeking to know and understand. Your creative juices will flood the whole world. The word 'joy' best sums up the celebration of life; of daring and caring despite the odds. Ganesha says home, house, work, status, prestige, parents, in-laws, travel will keep you on your 'twinkling toes' in 2018.

- **Element:** Earth
- **Ruling planet:** Mercury
- **Colours:** Earth tones, ochre, orange, yellow
- **Gems:** Agate, hyacinth (jacinth)

- **Metal:** Quicksilver
- **Scents:** Lavender, lilac, lily of the valley
- **Quality:** Mutability (=flexibility)
- **Quality most needed for balance:** A broader perspective
- **Strongest virtues:** Mental agility, analytical skills, ability to pay attention to detail, healing powers
- **Deepest needs:** To be useful and productive
- **Characteristics to avoid:** Destructive criticism
- **Day:** Wednesday
- **Number:** Five
- **Flowers:** Buttercup, pansy, forget-me-not, morning glory, aster, mimosa

- **Trees:** Hazel, horse chestnut, and all nut-bearing trees
- **Foods:** Potatoes, carrots, turnips, all vegetables grown under the earth; also nuts of all varieties

SPECIAL MESSAGE FROM BEJAN AND NASTUR

In ancient times Virgo, Libra and Scorpio were one sign. My special observation is that all these three signs are very choosy and fussy about food and health and may have phobias. I repeat that they *may* have phobias. I do not say that all of them have definite phobias. A Virgo woman is usually aware of health and hygiene issues, especially when it concerns cutting-edge research.

JUPITER

Jupiter will be in your third angle from 10 October 2017 to 8 November 2018. Jupiter stands for good luck, success and expansion. The additional goodies of Jupiter will be courage and valour, physical fitness, hobbies, talent, education, good qualities, longevity of parents, tolerance, capability, quality and nature of food, selfishness, sports, fights, refuge, trading, dreams, sorrows, stability of mind, the neighbourhood, near relations, friends, army, inheritance, ornaments, cleverness, short journeys. Wow! What a list!

The additional highlights are:

a) This is the right time to take crash course in matters which interest you, develop self-expression, and cultivate opinions.

b) Play chess or bridge, enter quiz shows, Sudoku contests, in short, all mental games.

c) Learn to get along with relatives and neighbours.

d) Try not to have mental strain, because this is where you are weak and therefore vulnerable; be ready to listen to others, though I know you are both able and discriminating.

e) Enrich your mind and enhance your knowledge.

I have mentioned this in earlier writings. Major climatic changes are happening, with dire consequences on our planet. Jupiter in third angle shows research, intelligence and thrust to help people realize that we are the family of man. Ganesha says, Jupiter in your third angle could help enhance memory and the processing of talk. More accurate weather/climate and geological predictions could perhaps be made too. Perhaps even artificial intelligence could be the final gift of Jupiter in the third angle. All these could be the brainchild or handiwork of your sign.

SATURN

Rationality and romance are born enemies. Why? Love is blind. The heart has its reasons which the mind never understands. But perhaps in your case there may be unique blending of romance and finance. I am writing it in the days of demonetization, namely, 9 December 2016.

By Western astrology, Saturn will be in your fifth angle from 21 December 2017 to 22 March 2020. The actual results of it will be:

1. Tremendous creativity;
2. A very wide choice in life.

Let us first take tremendous creativity. In this, the following features will be included:

a) pleasurable pursuits and hobbies;
b) children and other loved ones;

c) executive ability;

d) romance;

e) strengthening bonds of affection;

f) highlighting social activities;

g) seeing things in a new light, having faith in the future.

Ganesha says, Saturn in the fifth angle also gives pain, separation and shocks in the above matters. The home could be disturbed and disrupted. In short, Saturn will give you mixed results. Be ready to laugh and cry in the same breath.

You Virgos (and Geminis too) are experts in contacts and communication, each in his/her own way. Mercury is your boss planet. Mercury helps you in every possible way. From 1 to 17 January, 11 February to 6 March: journeys and religion; 31 March to 24 April: long-distance connections and ceremonies; 20 May to 13 June: combining home and work; 10 July to 6 August: confidence, courage, journeys, research; 9 September to 31 October: all-round personality like Virat Kohli. And once again, from 3 to 31 December: house, home, property. Let me make it very clear to you that this is only a general reading and therefore it will not apply completely and very accurately to you. If it does, consider it as Ganesha's grace.

URANUS

Uranus will move in and out of your health sector giving you mixed results. But if you have a chronic health problem it should go away by the end of 2019 latest. Reiki, dowsing, yoga, positive thinking, the use of colours, water therapy, mud bath, sauna bath – yes all these will help you in terms of wholeness and well-being.

NEPTUNE

Neptune will make your heart hum like a guitar and you might sing like a bird of paradise. After a time, there could be a few thorns in your throat also. Why? Neptune is both reality and illusion. But overall, Neptune will help you in terms of unusual partnerships, friends, romance, journeys. You are advised to stay away from drinks and drugs for your own good.

PLUTO

Pluto is the punch of the late Muhammad Ali, the world's greatest boxer. Pluto makes you glamorous, sexy, appealing and charming. Use it wisely and well.

MONTHLY ROUND-UP

January: You will be off and away to a really flying start, says Ganesha, and as you know, well begun is half done;

February and **March:** Expenses but also progress, therefore, mixed results;

April: Excellent for finances and family affairs and earned income;

May: Reaching out to people and places by all media of transport and communication;

June: Important for peace, buying/selling/renovating/decorating, a home away from home;

July: Love, romance, the luck of the draw, creativity and children, family and fun and fortune;

August: Health, employment, pets, servants and colleagues and a few problems connected with these;

September: Love and hate, marriage and making merry, but paradoxically, in a few cases, separation and legal cases, and that is why life is so complex, uncertain, full of contradictions and surprises;

October: Funds, loans, capital formation, money matters, shopping;

November: Inspiration, journeys, name and fame, good luck;

December: Power, prestige, parents, profession, awards and rewards, money, home, house and office.

HAPPINESS QUOTA: 87 per cent

WEEKLY REVIEW (BY PHASES OF THE MOON)

2 JANUARY: FULL MOON IN CANCER

You're upwardly mobile, most definitely so in terms of money, entertaining, social life. Gains in power, prestige, status too. Also, time for family outings, bonding with spouse and children and friends. There can be a tendency to overindulge in all pleasures of the flesh.

8 JANUARY: LAST QUARTER IN LIBRA

Careful handling of finances and some clever moves will maintain the upward trend of last week, in money matters and other spheres as well. You have a fine start to the year, Virgos, and it may prevail right through the year, barring a few hiccups, of course. It happens in all families and you'll take it in your stride.

17 JANUARY: NEW MOON IN CAPRICORN

You may be justified in thinking you've never had it so good. All the Ps – power, prestige, promotion, pelf, perks, position – are yours for the taking. And take them you will, believe me. As if these were not enough, there may even be romance, falling genuinely in love, if you're still young at heart and fancy-free.

24 JANUARY: FIRST QUARTER IN TAURUS

You've got more than your share to keep you busy and happy, but now there will be the added benefit of spirituality, religion, tantra and mantra. Your mind soars to new heights. Money matters will be good – collaborations, deals, mergers will click. A change of residence or job could be on the cards as part of the deal.

31 JANUARY: FULL MOON IN LEO

Secret matters, hushed negotiations, deals and behind-the-scene activities will definitely be there in some form or other. You will also be more withdrawn from the world, seeking out lonely places or at least, showing a desire for solitude. Contrarily enough, at the same time, a fair amount of travelling, business and professional interaction, meeting the right people and sparkling social interaction.

7 FEBRUARY: LAST QUARTER IN SCORPIO

Finances will suddenly be easy, so will the flow of cash for both domestic and office/business needs. There will be growth and expansion of work. Physically, health is somewhat better and there will be warmth in relationships, family ties, marital harmony too. All this because of your own inner growth and mentality, the readiness to reach out.

15 FEBRUARY: NEW MOON IN AQUARIUS

Work is in the spotlight, and you perform with your usual Virgo precision and efficiency. Novel ideas, avant-garde projects, even fresh collaborations will take off, and pending ones successfully completed. Ways and means of getting an extra income, making that extra buck, will come to you, in a flash of inspiration.

23 FEBRUARY: FIRST QUARTER IN GEMINI

You've got your eye on the main chance, all right, in your career or profession. A change of job, town or city, transfer or deputation to another department could well materialize. The change of scene could even be a promotion but there should be much advancement and progress in your career graph right now.

2 MARCH: FULL MOON IN VIRGO

Your public image and private persona shine forth like a newly minted coin. It's your profession/job/career/business that you'll shine the most in, though some of the glitter rubs off on to family life as well. You will be a true representative of the success and dynamism that most people aspire for these days.

9 MARCH: LAST QUARTER IN SAGITTARIUS

It's your family, your roots, that are important for you, and your home is the centre of the universe, in that sense. Parents, in-laws and older relatives will have your care and attention lavished on them, as also the house and home, despite a certain amount of time spent away from it in travel.

17 MARCH: NEW MOON IN PISCES

You go all out to realize your ambition and make future plans a reality, both professionally and domestically. And you're on the brink of achieving it all, this week, if not already there in some ways. Of course, the temptation to overdo things, take on more than you can cope with is to be avoided, and rest and relaxation will be more necessary than ever.

24 MARCH: FIRST QUARTER IN CANCER

It's warm companionship, togetherness and love that warm the cockles of your heart this week and you're not just in the mood to relax but to party and socialize as well. Virgos can often be party animals. At any rate, they need hectic social life, interaction with friends and even acquaintances to feel they're really alive. And you're no exception.

31 MARCH: FULL MOON IN LIBRA

The two Fs of family and finance are still the main focus. Some family matters will need to be disentangled on an urgent basis right now, though they've been on the back burner while you were caught up with work and career demands. These issues could well pertain to family, money or property. You will be in a daring mood in business transactions and money matters.

8 APRIL: LAST QUARTER IN CAPRICORN

You see-saw between the world of material things and that of relationships, so this time it's ties, bonds, relationships once again. It's a happy time in terms of outings, entertainment, luck investments, creativity in hobbies and specially in your joy from your children. The extra bonus will be the total commitment and joy from that special someone in your life/heart – your true love.

16 APRIL: NEW MOON IN ARIES

You'll be almost hyperactive in both work and recreation in equal measure. It's a time for risk taking for both love and money. Two time-tested sayings – 'Fortune favours the brave' and 'Faint heart never won fair lady' just about sum up this quarter for Virgos. Also, a bit of socializing, a dash of travel, and hectic activity all round!

22 APRIL: FIRST QUARTER IN LEO

On the work front, your public relations and people skills will be mind-boggling. You will achieve targets easily, meet deadlines, accomplish difficult missions and assignments with deceptive ease. You'll get on 'swimmingly' with people, as Bertie Wooster would have said, and that is the secret of your success.

30 APRIL: FULL MOON IN SCORPIO

There'll be expenses that go off into the outer hemisphere, they're so high, but income will match, so there could, really speaking, be no money worries. Part of the expenses could well be gadgets, comforts and luxuries for the home, that is equally in focus this quarter. A phase that you should be thankful for has prevailed for you for the last few weeks.

8 MAY: LAST QUARTER IN AQUARIUS

There's no stopping you while you're on a roll, as Saurav Ganguly was when he broke the record at the World Cup League match at Taunton, England. Distinguished gatherings, PR exercises, friends in high places, and in the highest (political?) circles will ensure that nothing can stop your meteoric rise.

15 MAY: NEW MOON IN TAURUS

Journeys will yield pleasure and profit, so too will romance, marriage, or getting married – more pleasure, I'm not so sure about profit! Your public image will shine forth. Conferences, meets, seminars, collaborations will have you participating brilliantly, and having a whale of a time doing it. More power to you, says Ganesha's devotee.

22 MAY: FIRST QUARTER IN VIRGO

Secret deals, closed-door meetings, arcane and esoteric activities and pursuits will be most important in this period. A secret love affair or liaison, perhaps, also. With this kind of cloak-and-dagger stuff, and hidden romance, your expenses will be very high indeed. It's expensive to have mistresses or play cops and robbers, isn't it?

29 MAY: FULL MOON IN SAGITTARIUS

You will throw out all the excitement and high living from your lifestyle and concentrate on home and family, a quiet life, the joys of domesticity and slippers warming on the hearth. You're still a daring risk taker in matters financial, though, and investments and speculation will be very, very lucrative.

6 JUNE: LAST QUARTER IN PISCES

To make all your ambitions and dreams a reality, you'll have to work your butt off! And you're able and willing, this period. Travel with a stopover, maybe, and ties and collaborations. There will be heightened activity in this period since it's in your birth sign. What will also be majorly important will be partnerships, whether old or new, professional or personal.

13 JUNE: NEW MOON IN GEMINI

You'll be impressive at work, in your office/factory/business premises. It's at your workplace that you're at your best this week, though even at play and pleasure pursuits, you come a close second. There is a certain intensity in all that you undertake. Whatever, you make all the right moves, say and do all the right things, with Ganesha's inspiration.

20 JUNE: FIRST QUARTER IN VIRGO

It's a phase when you want to review your life, reassess your values, priorities and focus, even while you continue to work without letting up on your standards. It's your home and family that get your attention, and there may be an intensely personal matter to resolve as well. A long-cherished dream may come true now.

28 JUNE: FULL MOON IN CAPRICORN

In this period the glitter and sparkle are even more wonderful. Here's how it goes: a) achievements – advertising, the arts, information technology, research, academics all do brilliantly; b) happiness in personal life – laughter, good friends, romance, love and marriage; c) success – good partnerships, deals made now are crowned with great profit and gain.

6 JULY: LAST QUARTER IN ARIES

Home and family may need some reorganizing. You will need a lot of funds for domestic affairs, so joint finance, marital funds and accounts will have to be dealt with, along with career demands. There may be a financial settlement to be made and domestic responsibilities to be fulfilled. You need not shelve your own individual career aspirations to do so.

13 JULY: NEW MOON IN CANCER

It's a time for not money, or monetary gain, but truly hitting the jackpot in life, in terms of both advancement and wealth, serious money. You will have it all – power, position, prestige and pelf. Ganesha's bounty will have no limits for you, at least in material terms.

19 JULY: FIRST QUARTER IN LIBRA

You'll have to pack more activity into this phase of your life than ever before, and the main thrust, focus, goal and result, will be money. The colour of money influences all your activities, at home, in the office, even with pets and children and certainly love and romance and marriage, not to mention your social life.

27 JULY: FULL MOON IN AQUARIUS

A trend of sheer, mind-blowing hard work is coupled with equally mind-blowing success in love, romance, moneymaking. In addition, you'll be drawn to religion, tantra and mantra, prayer and meditation for rest, relaxation and inspiration. Even success can be tiring, as I'm sure you'll be discovering by now. This will be the trend for the next few weeks.

4 AUGUST: LAST QUARTER IN TAURUS

It's socializing with a bang, panache and style. You will truly have a ball this week. Business and public relations, ceremonies and functions, parties, games and sports, ties and collaborations. You also make money in the bargain! But rest, health care and an improved routine, and diet will prove to be more necessary than ever.

11 AUGUST: NEW MOON IN LEO

Dealing with sickness, visits to the hospitals – for yourself or someone close to you – will make you stop in your tracks and think. So also will the mind-boggling expenses. It could be that you have not heeded my warning of last week. In any case, you will want to reassess the way your life is going, wonderful as it may be, and try for a different focus or goal and a more laid-back approach.

18 AUGUST: FIRST QUARTER IN SCORPIO

There will be a remarkable coming together of family members in your scheme of things. Your brothers, sisters, close relatives will mean much to you. There will be a fair amount of travel and expansion of the mind – learning a new skill, computer technology, higher study, research, further qualifications. This will all prove to be a more or less direct result of the last week's soul-searching.

26 AUGUST: FULL MOON IN PISCES

A period of intense activity. This is usual in the birth month of all signs. There will be skills and achievements galore, some dreams coming true, ambitions realized but this kind of dazzling success that you have enjoyed since May excites envy, jealousy, even enmity in others. You will need to watch out, particularly in money matters where you must *not,* repeat *not,* go anywhere near doubtful, fraudulent deals.

3 SEPTEMBER: LAST QUARTER IN GEMINI

It is only now that the necessity of being prepared for any eventuality makes you appreciate the worth of true values, good motives and righteous living. It's not that you haven't done so earlier, but now it becomes a part of your life in a way never before experienced, even by you, perfection-loving Virgo. Your commitment to hard work continues and is built in to this approach to life.

9 SEPTEMBER: NEW MOON IN VIRGO

Caring, sharing, attachments, peace, excellence, harmony – all come together for you. Your family, loved ones, and particularly your spouse, will be 'the be-all and end-all' of your life. I can't express it better than in this famous phrase of William Shakespeare's. This conviction will guide all your actions and activities, even love and romance in the future.

16 SEPTEMBER: FIRST QUARTER IN SAGITTARIUS

You will be truly original, inventive and ingenious in your approach to life and living, even New Age living. The home and hearth, your own property or piece of earth, will come in for renovation, restoration, care. You will be marvellous too at all kinds of communication, but most of all in family issues where you display wisdom tempered with affection.

25 SEPTEMBER: FULL MOON IN ARIES

A tremendous burst of power, greatness and glory. It will be centred around religion, money, sex and passion – perhaps all of them! This is a time when you are a winner in the game of life, but have to pay for the chips you gamble with. Health worries, the slight changes because of an accident may need to be watched out for, warns Ganesha.

2 OCTOBER: LAST QUARTER IN CANCER

You will experience a letting up of the tensions and worries that come to you. You will relax, rejuvenate yourself. (This can be done at any age.) Good company, friends, socializing, merrymaking and laughter, outings and sports – all these activities contribute in no small measure. Added to this will be success in business/profession.

9 OCTOBER: NEW MOON IN LIBRA

The three Fs – food, family and of course, finance. But here they need a little explaining. Let's start with: a) Food – implying entertaining and being entertained, dining out, the hospitality industry, even diet care, hotels, restaurants, nutrition consultation; b) Family – matters not involving just your immediate family and siblings, but also extended family, in-laws, your ancestors, your roots and your attachment to them.

16 OCTOBER: FIRST QUARTER IN CAPRICORN

It will be just people for you this period. Personal relationships are everything to you, right now. These will necessarily show complete involvement in your individual worth and creativity, your children's affairs, activities, pursuits and finally domestic and family issues. All of these will be important to you, and your role in them will be equally important and vital. That's it.

24 OCTOBER: FULL MOON IN TAURUS

The trend which set in with the last new moon phase extends over and into this month as well. Wish-fulfilment, dreams coming true; a total self-improvement campaign from clothes and hairstyle to home. Also important will be journeys and ceremonies – religious and otherwise, and of course, the best for the last – fireworks in terms of intuition, perception, strokes of pure genius.

31 OCTOBER: LAST QUARTER IN LEO

Journeys and relationships are most important for you. With travel comes a certain distancing yourself from this world you live in, a touch of world-weariness, ennui, disillusionment. It's only the reaching out to places and people that will help you overcome this, as well as the sense of aloneness that could overwhelm you. Ganesha will give you solace – he always does.

7 NOVEMBER: NEW MOON IN SCORPIO

You have put the past quarter's phase behind you, performing brilliantly at interviews, examinations, tests of skill and/or mental agility and ability. There's much happiness from your children too to pull you out of the doldrums and finally, lots of travel as well. You do it all with typical Virgo thoroughness and excellence.

15 NOVEMBER: FIRST QUARTER IN AQUARIUS

Money matters and those concerning dependents will be where you try out your impressive skills at management, the attempt to put the entire world in order. Money matters will relate to loans and funds for projects, arranging for capital, investments for social work in particular. Social ills and anomalies will be attacked head-on by you now.

23 NOVEMBER: FULL MOON IN GEMINI

Perks, promotions, prospects, position and power are the five Ps from now till the end of 2018. That's the millennium's gift to you, all given a kick-start but showing results now. Respect, recognition, rewards, they're all there. Learn to be grateful, says Ganesha and don't criticize others not so lucky as you are. Nothing succeeds like success, they say, but kindness to less successful people succeeds even more.

30 NOVEMBER: LAST QUARTER IN VIRGO

There will be a lot of idealism in your attitudes now, particularly regarding the values of self-help and hard work and sheer striving for excellence. All of which are a necessary part of your personality and mental make-up. You'll incorporate all of this in your life in 'the daily round, the common task' and lift beyond the ordinary.

7 DECEMBER: NEW MOON IN SAGITTARIUS

A new line of work, alongside your own, that you had undertaken earlier in the year, could prove to be more absorbing and interesting. So also your public image, how others see you, how you project yourself to the whole wide world. Your inner self will remain largely hidden, especially the lofty ideals and sentiments that you have acquired. It's only to a chosen few that you show your true self, or let down your guard.

15 DECEMBER: FIRST QUARTER IN PISCES

You'll hold out the olive branch to your enemies, get in touch with long-lost relatives, long-forgotten friends and visit childhood haunts in a trip down memory lane. People will be important, if not everything now as you build bridges of entente cordiale. So also will love and romance – cosy twosomes against the chill of winter! Official and private functions and ceremonies will keep you busy, and happy too.

22 DECEMBER: FULL MOON IN CANCER

You will have all the three cardinal virtues of faith, hope and charity in your heart as you look at 2,000 years of the Christian era. Also, a look ahead at the dawn of the next 1,000 years of enlightenment, hope for the future and a better world order. It's not idle thoughts and hopes though. You're ready to roll up your sleeves and get ready to work to make it all happen. More power to you, my brother in mankind, say Ganesha and I.

29 DECEMBER: LAST QUARTER IN LIBRA

The euphoria generated by your achievements, activities, honour and reputation, now brings tremendous gains in terms of both warm friendship and material advancement, so that you feel fulfilled, satisfied, pleased with life. It is however, a time to steer clear of involvement in money matters with friends, associates or colleagues. All in all, you will be more friendly, more magnanimous, but also more extravagant.

Achievements 2018

By the grace of Lord Ganesh, my son Nastur found patrons in Shri Raj Kumar Jatia and his son, Shri Adarsh Jatia, the owners of Four Seasons, Mumbai, and Provenance Four Seasons Private Residences. May patience and hard work take my son to the top of the world where Shri Raj Kumar Jatia stands like a shining star. Nastur was graciously invited by the noble business tycoon, Byram Avari, of Avari Group of Hotels, Karachi, and his wife, Goshpi Avari, to attend their fiftieth wedding anniversary.

I bless prosperity upon Prayush Poddar, his father and his family. May his company, AMP Universal Realty Pvt. Ltd, prosper. He has been like a son to me.

May the grace of Lord Ganesha bless Police Commissioner Anupam Singh Gehlot of Rajkot. He has always stood by my family, in good times and bad. Peace and prosperity prevail in Rajkot because of his sincere efforts.

BJP National vice-president and Rajya Sabha member, Vinay Sahasrabuddhe is a very fine and noble gentleman. He was gracious enough to arrange a meeting with Maharashtra chief minister Devendra Fadnavis, who was dynamic and touched by the divine.

Body Language

Ganesha believed astrology to be all about behaviour, relationships and how to handle them. Therefore, the guidelines given below should help you to understand yourself and others. Any information that adds to the knowledge of oneself is always welcome. Here are some examples of body language and its possible interpretations:

POSITIVE VIBES

- Open arms and hands: open and receptive
- Leaning forward: interested in conversation

- Smiling or attempting to be humorous: friendly
- Eye contact with occasional, natural breaks in the stare: focused and curious
- Nodding while listening: attentive and alert
- Open palms: approachable and trusting
- Gesturing with hands while talking: genuinely involved in the conversation
- Upright shoulders: positivity

NEGATIVE VIBES

- Crossed arms and/or legs: closed off, defensive, reserved or suspicious
- Standing with hands inside the pockets: unsure or suspicious
- Fidgeting, running one's tongue along one's teeth, playing with hair

or jewellery or tapping feet: nervous and/or bored

- Lack of eye contact or staring too intently and unblinkingly: untrustworthy
- Leaning back: uncomfortable
- Clasping hands behind the head while leaning back: seeking power
- Drooping shoulders: unsure

Colours of Life

Ganesha believes that life is like a rainbow. Life is like nature, full of abundance and variety. The best part of it is you can actually experiment with the colours given below and have fun. Here, we combine abundance and a variety of colours for joy, use, experience.

- **Energetic:** Red
- **Sporty:** Red, orange
- **Exuberant:** Orange
- **Active:** Orange, yellow
- **Modern:** Yellow

- **Invigorating:** Green, yellow
- **Sunny:** Green, yellow
- **Fresh:** Green
- **Luminous:** Blue, Green
- **Hypnotic:** Blue
- **Regal:** Blue, violet
- **Exotic:** Violet
- **Playful:** Red, orange, violet, yellow
- **Vibrant:** Green, red

(Your astrologer admits that this colour system is *not* his own.)

Important Dates

I have always believed that the fear of failure has never led to advancement of knowledge. These dates and directions may differ from the various trends and forecasts mentioned elsewhere in the book. A different direction is being pursued here. This is a totally different ball game. This is to be taken as an experiment on a mass scale with the readers themselves as guinea pigs (willingly, I hope).

Please remember, as a rule, your birth month and the seventh month from it (including itself) will be hectic. For example, if your birth month is March, the seventh from it will be September. There will be tremendous franticness in both these months.

January: 1–2, 5–7, 10–12, 15–16, 19–20, 23–24, 28–29

February: 2–3, 7–8, 11–12, 16–17, 20–21, 24–26, 29

March: 1–2, 5–6, 10–11 14–15, 18–19, 22–24, 27–29

April: 1–3, 6–7, 10–11, 14–16, 19–20, 24–25, 29–30

May: 3–4, 7–8, 12–13, 16–18, 21–23, 26–27, 31

June: 1, 4–5, 8–9, 12–14, 17–19, 22–23, 27–28

July: 1–2, 6–7, 10–12, 15–16, 20–21, 24–26, 29–30

August: 2–3, 6–7, 11–13, 16–18, 21–22, 25–26, 29–31

September: 2–4, 7–9, 12–14, 17–18, 21–22, 25–26, 30

October: 1, 4–6, 9–11, 14–15, 18–20, 23–26 (very important), 30–31

November: 1–2, 6–7, 10–12, 15–16, 19–20, 23–25, 28–30

December: 3–5, 8–9, 12–13, 16–17, 20–24, 26–27 30–31

Special Note: The reason, dear Virgos, for so many important dates in January is that you will start the year in style. You will have the advantage of being in the fast lane of love, life and laughter. See that your tentacles catch and hold on to all those you can count on. Children will give you immense satisfaction. This March, you will travel and touch the lives of people. Importantly, you will drop your guard and shed your inhibitions. In May, despite delays and hesitations, your heart will sympathize and be in symphony with others. This is the time to plan your future. The people you meet in your working life will influence you the most is June. July is the meeting point of home and the outside wide world of privacy and group activity. For Virgos, September will be a great month. You move into top gear on 23 October. The last days of December find you fit, charming, romantic and, more importantly, willing to take chances.

Secret of Life

Ganesha (whom you may refer to as Allah/Christ/Zoroaster or by any other name) is the ignition key of life's car. To start and launch in the name of Ganesha is to assure success and glory. The power, the dazzling light to see visions, have prophetic dreams, and are all bestowed upon us by Ganesha.

Ganesha says the secret of life is in the ability to change with the changing times. In other words, it is the ability to adapt and adjust to situations, conditions, surroundings, climate change, relationships, and science and technology. His second secret is to keep an open mind. Others are most welcome to their own opinion. The third and final secret is to be true to yourself.

Success Secret of No. 17

Ganesha says the secret of life and astrology is to 'Observe! Observe! Observe!' Angela Merkel of Germany, our own Narendra Modi, former US first lady Michelle Obama, and Muhammad Ali, the world's greatest boxer, were all born on the seventeenth days of their birth months. Here is a picture of the tarot card of number seventeen, called the 'Star'. We can see a lady pouring water on the Earth and providing nourishment. To me the lady is the symbol of the great feminine principle which rules the entire world. There are seven stars in the card. As we all know, seven is the mystical number of spirituality, growth and development.

Narendra Modi, 17 September

Michelle Obama, 17 January

Angela Merkel, 17 July

Muhammad Ali, 17 January

To observe is to see completely and carefully. If you observe the above, you will find that all these four individuals are born on the seventeenth. Secondly, the first alphabet of either the first name or the surname in each case is 'M'. The tarot card points towards a great and powerful destiny. Therefore, for all these reasons I believe that the number seventeen and the letter 'M' go with greatness and glory. Yes, I agree that it may not hold true for all the persons born on the seventeenth of various months. I am open-minded.

Is it but a coincidence or is it fate and destiny? I leave it to you to decide.

World Horoscope 2018

Ganesha says cooking is an art. The challenge lies in the ever-changing nature of the ingredients, the temperature, the flavour, the aroma and the very style of cooking.

The ingredients are: artificial intelligence; healing broken bodies, mind, and spirit (most important); managerial skills of a high order; immense strides in medicine and specially brain power; space travel; robots; biopharmaceuticals; origin of life; God vs technology; climate change; and finally the marriage of technology and humanity.

Let me put it in very simple terms. The years from 2018 to 2020 will have both revolution and evolution. Change is the only constant law of nature. Not only will we survive, we will also prevail. The planets responsible for this constant change in direction are Jupiter, Saturn and Pluto. Jupiter means prosperity, Saturn means inevitable changes and Pluto means drastic and unavoidable situations and effects. These three planets are the trio of the cardinal, ambitious, ruthless sign of duty and responsibility: Capricorn. In short, Capricorn is the father who uses a big stick for others but unhappily not for himself. That is the comedy and the tragedy of the Capricorn sign.

As I have said earlier, this is not the right time for Donald Trump. His world view is one that is corrupted by imagination, illusion and, sometimes, hallucination. The Capricorn North Korean President Kim Jong-un will face terrible times and will be completely defeated in the end by fate. Vladimir Putin of Russia and Theresa May of the UK will find it very difficult to hold on to power. Angela Merkel of Germany is simply wonderful and effective. There is a distinct possibility of a settlement or an understanding between the Jews and the Muslims in 2018 itself. God bless them both. Changes in the regimes in Pakistan and the UK appear certain. In the words of Paul Brenton, 'There is peace behind the tumult, goodness behind the evil, happiness behind the agony.' Nobody has a monopoly over truth, love, justice, mercy, kindness and happiness.

India is certainly tolerant up to a certain extent, but it would be wise, practical and necessary to be much more tolerant and far less rigid and orthodox. Water recycling and the treatment of sewage will be a big changer for our country in 2018 and 2019. It will lead to happiness. I say this in all humility and love for Bharat Mata as I am her child. I certainly bow my head at the feet of Bharat Mata. India comes under the planet of Saturn causing changes that are radical, effective, certain. Our Narendra Modi will hold his own against the world. But India will undergo numerous changes, a few of them could be painful but are necessary in the bigger scheme of events. Not religion but responsibility, duty and development will be the three salient features of India in the coming years.

To be happy we must keep an open mind. Perhaps, I say perhaps the best years will be 2018 and 2021. The year 2021 is most certainly the one when science and technology reign supreme and change the very fabric and direction of all of us. Possibly this is the greatest prediction your humble Ganesha devotee will ever make.

Salute and Tribute

A salute and tribute to the following people:

- Gujarat chief minister Vijay Rupani, in whom I saw a perfect balance in the lines of fate, head and heart on his palms. A great heart and a finely tuned mind.
- Philanthropist and naturalist Firdoz Khambhatta, a dangerously handsome, sharp and brilliant man.
- The lovely Meher Medora, firm of purpose and understanding and sympathetic of heart.

- Aravind Mothi and his sister, Anu Mothi, for offering to make a documentary on my life.
- Hotelier Raj Kumar Jatia for his hospitality and courtesy.
- Behram Mehta for his business acumen fused with immense humility and humanity.
- Jay Shah, son of BJP president Amit Shah, for coming to my house and seeking the blessings of all the mighty spirits and energies of each and every religion.
- The very cultured, civilized, and well-informed education minister of Gujarat, Shri Bhupendra Chudasma for his wisdom as well as his faith in Ganesha.
- Usha Nair, Dr Sunny Shah, Nashit Afroze and their team at the International Human Rights Council for services rendered to NGOs all

over the world. I was very humbled to receive a trophy from them, one I shall always treasure.

- Prince Lakshyaraj of Udaipur for his constant endeavour to help thousands of people through education, NGOs and by example for leading an exemplary life.
- My personal blessings by calling upon all the energies of the world to bless my adopted son Chirag and his fiancée Nikita. They are gems.
- I bow very humbly to my guru, Vashishth Mehta, for coaching me across the path of astrology and spirituality.
- Kudos to Neeraj Bajaj, the son of my late friend and patron Ramkrishna Bajaj, and Dadi Mistry for helping the needy, the weak and the helpless in every possible way. Both are truly magnanimous people.

- Raja Vikram Singh of Jambughoda for his humour and resounding laughter. No wonder his Jambughoda resort is doing immensely well.
- Just as this book is going to press, I met Shiroy and his fiancée, Avasti. Avasti specializes in fashion. Shiroy is an absolute gentleman.
- Lastly, I salute and pay my tribute to all those who seek and serve the cause of peace and goodwill to humanity. To me this is certainly the final word.

About the Author

Born on 11 July 1931, Bejan Daruwalla lives with his wife and their three children. Now, eighty-six years old, he is regarded as one of the hundred greatest astrologers of the last century, as acknowledged by *The Millennium Book of Prophecy* (HarperCollins), having accurately predicted the electoral victory of Narendra Modi at the Kanoria Art Centre, Ahmedabad, on 29 March 2012. Bejan featured on *Hard Talk India* on BBC in August 1999. On 10 December 2010, Bejan was featured in *The Job: Corporate Astrologer* in London's *Financial Times*. Bejan was also awarded the Dr Babasaheb Ambedkar Noble Award on 19 April 2017. Giving Bejan more joy and material achievement was shaking hands with His Holiness the Dalai Lama in December 2013, a moment unforgotten and overwhelming. Bejan has one firm belief: tolerance. He believes everyone has the right to their own ideas and opinions; the perspective of others, even and especially if it differs from one's own, must always be respected.

Important Announcement

Our Ganesha devotee Bejan Daruwalla has moved from Mumbai to Ahmedabad. His Ahmedabad address is:

Bejan Daruwalla
Astrologer and Columnist
C/o Nastur Daruwalla
A-5, Spectrum Towers
Opposite Police Stadium
Shahibag
Ahmedabad 380004
India

Telephone

079-32954387

09825470377

08141234275

Email

info@bejandaruwalla.com

bejandaruwalla@rediffmail.com

Website: www.bejandaruwalla.com